SUPER WHO? SUPER ME!

Written by Jo Darby
Illustrated by Aimee Del Valle

First edition March 2021

© of the words: Jo Darby
© of the illustrations: Aimee Del Valle

All rights reserved. This book or any portion thereof may not be reproduced or used in any manner whatsoever without the express written permission of the author except for the use of brief quotations in a book review.

To Leo and Lola,

I aspire to be a better person every day
because your little eyes are watching me.
Just like I tell you before you sleep every night,
you can do anything you put your
mind to. You have greatness within.
Mummy x

Sunshine rises and sleepy eyes open,
let's feel super grateful and bring some hope in.

So many things to be grateful for,
like my house, my bed....

...and the world outside my door.

Stand in front of a mirror and you will see you have everything inside you that you need to be.

Hands on hips, I stand so tall,

I'm just like a **super hero** so hear me call.....

"I am..........brave

I am...........kind

I am happy inside my mind."

Eat your food and
really taste
every mouthful so none
goes to waste.
I'll enjoy every bite and eat
nice and slow,
because food is so fun when you're in the flow!

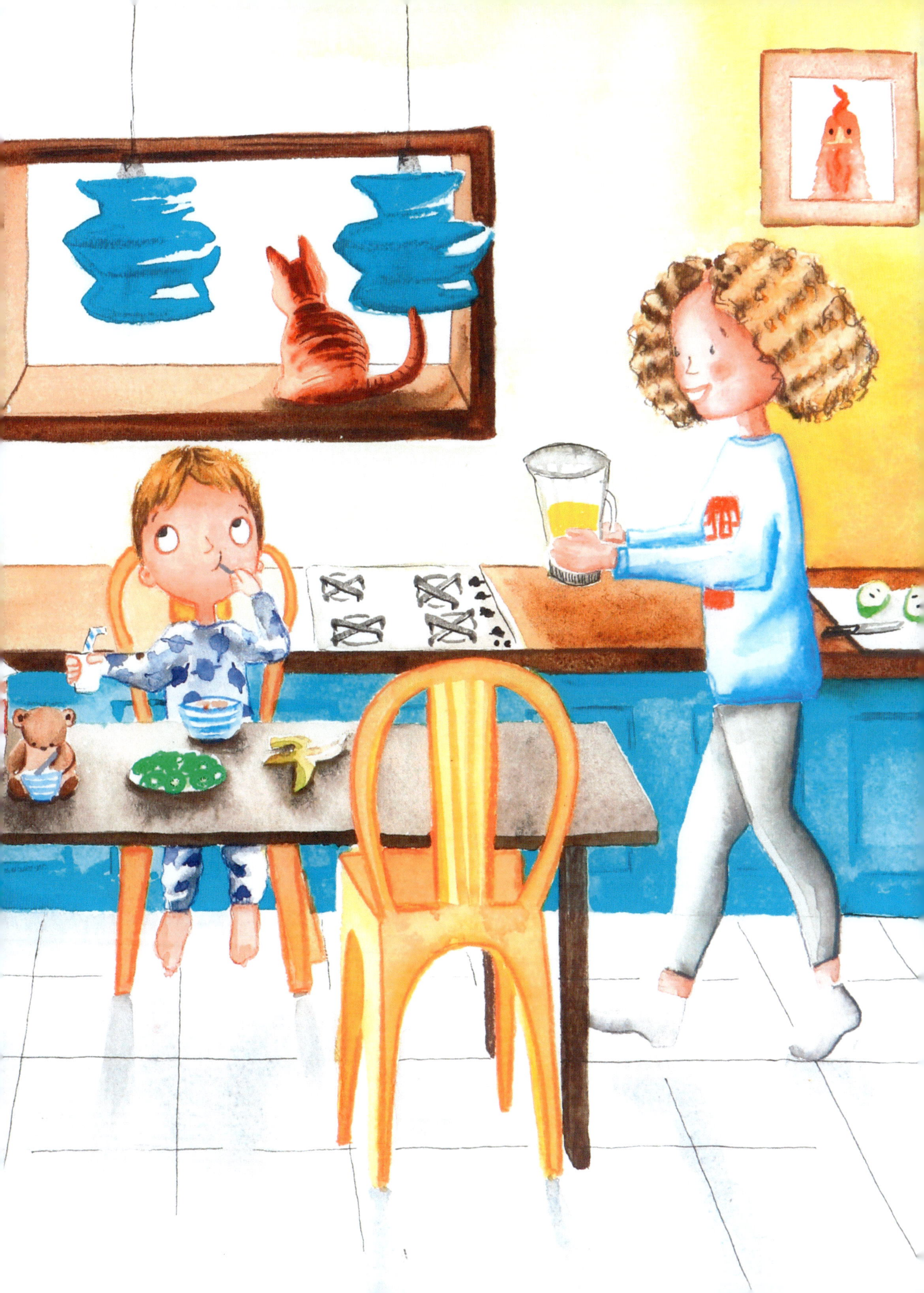

Time to get dressed and pull up those socks, can you move quickly and beat the clock?

I sing along.... "My body is made of cell after cell, they're happy and smiley and feeling so well."

Scooter or bike, bus or car,
it's fun to travel, whether it's near or far!

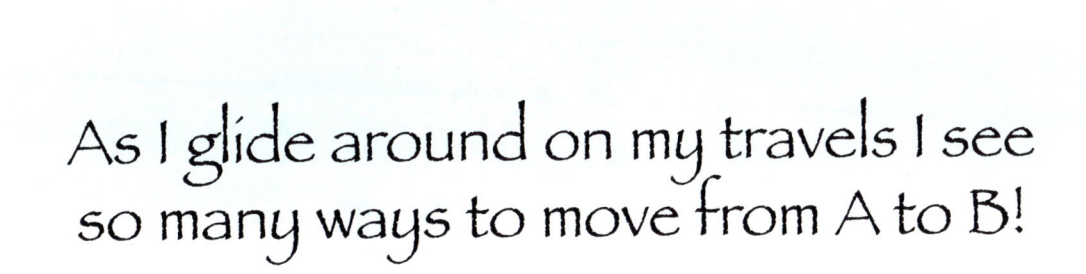

As I glide around on my travels I see
so many ways to move from A to B!

Each day you play and learn and read,
you're like an Oak, growing tall from a seed.
The things I do, whether big or small,
I focus and breathe and give it my all.

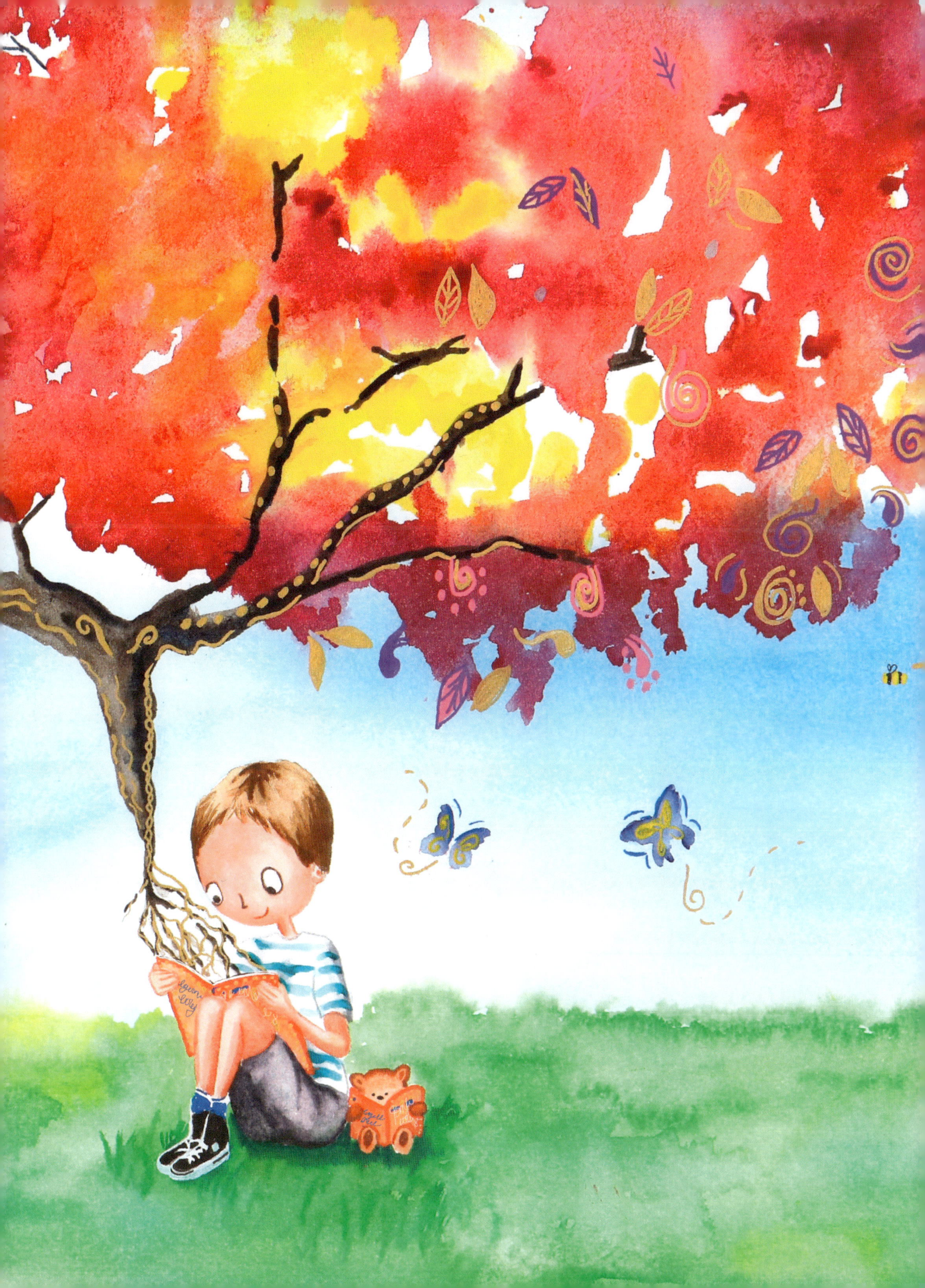

If you're feeling angry and aren't sure what to do,
blow away a cloud with all the mad inside of you.

If I ever feel angry or scared or just sad,
I take a big breath and blow out the bad.

If you see someone else with worries on their mind,

you can help by chatting and showing that you're kind.

Next time I see someone who looks a bit sad,
I'll ask them to play so they don't feel so bad.

Move your body every day because a healthy body means...

...more energy to play

I run

or dance

or skip

or hop

Because exercise is great
so I feel

tip top!

Sitting still
can you imagine a balloon
getting bigger and bigger inside your room?
I cross my legs and close my eyes,
take 5 big breaths and....

watch the balloon rise!

Before you sleep and dream away...

think of the best thing that happened that day!
What a magical day, I've laughed and twirled,
more adventures tomorrow...

...in this wonderful world.

KIND KIDZ

Kindness starts with me

For more inspiration and resources come and find us at www.kind-kidz.com and instagram @kind.kidz

Printed in Great Britain
by Amazon